To Hans and Christoph, my two true foodies.—W.S.

For all kids, everywhere.—C.E.

STERLING CHILDREN'S BOOKS
New York

An Imprint of Sterling Publishing Co., Inc.
1166 Avenue of the Americas
New York, NY 10036

ISBN 978-1-4549-2672-6

Distributed in Canada by Sterling Publishing Co., Inc.
c/o Canadian Manda Group, 664 Annette Street
Toronto, Ontario M6S 2C8, Canada
Distributed in the United Kingdom by GMC Distribution Services
Castle Place, 166 High Street, Lewes, East Sussex BN7 1XU, England
Distributed in Australia by NewSouth Books
45 Beach Street, Coogee NSW 2034, Australia

For information about custom editions, special sales, and premium and corporate purchases,
please contact Sterling Special Sales at 800-805-5489 or specialsales@sterlingpublishing.com.

Manufactured in China

Lot #:
2 4 6 8 10 9 7 5 3 1

12/17

sterlingpublishing.com

Cover and interior design by Heather Kelly

Photo credits—see page 33

WHAT'S ON YOUR PLATE?

Exploring the World of Food

by Whitney Stewart

illustrated by Christiane Engel

STERLING CHILDREN'S BOOKS

New York

Corn

Hummus

Tacos

Tortilla de Patates

Injera

EATING ACROSS LAND AND SEA

Have you ever noticed how food brings people together? Think of all the birthday parties and holiday gatherings you've attended with family—and think about the food that was served! The world over, people rejoice with feasts. In some countries, people welcome summer with a barbecue and corn on the cob. In others, people celebrate the New Year with a giant pot of noodle soup.

The foods we eat and the ways we cook them are part of what we call our *food culture*. Throughout the world, people have unique food cultures that are connected to the history and geography of where they live. In this book, we're going to explore those connections.

Imagine you are a voyager traveling from country to country, trying all the foods each one has to offer. Are you hungry? Get ready to find out what's cooking around the world, and taste it in your own kitchen.

⚠ A NOTE BEFORE YOU COOK ⚠

Cooking is fun, but accidents can happen if you're not careful. It's important to protect yourself when you're working with sharp knives or hot pots and pans. Ask an adult first before using kitchen tools. You can find kid-safe cooking tools at kitchen stores and online.

UNITED STATES

The first people to arrive on the land we now call the United States migrated from Asia more than ten thousand years ago. Their descendants lived in different groups called tribes. Some tribes, like the Wampanoag and Abenaki, grew corn, squash, and beans. They called this combination the "Three Sisters" because the plants grew together, with the bean plants winding around the corn stalks. Besides growing these key vegetables, tribes also harvested wild rice, which they often prepared and served with nuts, berries, and maple syrup. They roasted meat and seafood over an open fire.

Later, when colonists from Europe arrived on the land, they depended on the tribes for survival. The Wampanoag tribe taught the English Pilgrims of Plymouth Colony how to grow the Three Sisters, and in 1621, the Pilgrims and the Wampanoag feasted together on fish, wild bird, cornbread, and even popcorn. In the United States, people honor the event and celebrate this feast as a national holiday—Thanksgiving!

In the hundreds of years since then, immigrants from all over the world have come to America and have brought their favorite foods with them! Italians introduced pizza and pasta. Japanese people introduced sushi. Some of the most popular dishes in America today originated in other countries.

POPULAR AMERICAN FOODS

BARBECUED RIBS: pork ribs coated in sauce and grilled

CHEESEBURGER: chopped beef patty, grilled or fried, with melted cheese on top

FRIED CHICKEN: chicken pieces dipped in batter and fried

MASHED POTATOES: potatoes boiled and then mashed with milk and butter

CORN ON THE COB: CORN GRILLED OR BOILED
(2 servings)

INGREDIENTS
- Corn on the cob, 2 ears
- Salt
- Pepper
- Butter

INSTRUCTIONS
- Remove the husk and silky threads from the corn.
- Boil a large pot of water. Gently drop corn into the boiling water.
- Cover the pot and let the water come back to a boil.
- Turn off the heat. After five minutes carefully remove the corn with tongs.
- Smear with butter and add salt and pepper to taste.

Cheeseburger

Mashed Potatoes

Fried Chicken

MEXICO

Maize (corn) is at the heart of Mexican cuisine. The native people of Mexico soaked and boiled maize kernels in wood ash or lime. By doing this, they could easily remove the skin from the kernels. Then they pounded the maize into masa (flour) and shaped it into flat discs called tortillas. They baked the tortillas on hot stones and ate them with locally grown foods like beans, tomatoes, chili peppers, squash, and avocados. They also ate fish and wild turkey.

When Spanish conquerors arrived in Mexico in 1519, they introduced such new foods as wheat, pork, chicken, cheese, rice, and onions, all of which are still part of Mexican cuisine. Today people pile tortillas high with shredded meat, fish, and vegetables. These delicious folded tortillas are often served with salsa. Chances are, you've eaten them before—they're called tacos!

POPULAR MEXICAN FOODS

EMPANADAS (em-pa-NA-das): pastry filled with meat and vegetables, baked or fried

ENCHILADAS (en-chee-LA-das): rolled corn tortillas stuffed with vegetables or shredded meat, smothered in sauce, and baked

TACOS (TA-cohs): corn or flour tortillas filled with meat or fish and vegetables

TAMALES (ta-MA-lays): cornmeal paste stuffed with meat and vegetables, wrapped in a corn husk or banana leaf, and steamed

GUACAMOLE (gu-wa-ca-MOH-lay): AVOCADO DIP
(2 servings)

INGREDIENTS
- 1 large ripe avocado
- 1/4 cup chopped tomato
- 1/4 cup minced onion
- 1/4 cup chopped cilantro
- 1 tablespoon fresh lime juice (optional)
- Salt to taste

INSTRUCTIONS
- Cut the avocado in half. Discard the pit and scoop the fruit into a bowl.
- Using a fork or blender, mash avocado to a paste.
- Add the chopped tomato, minced onion, and chopped cilantro.
- Add lime juice and salt.
- Continue mashing until smooth.
- Serve with chips or on a tortilla.

Tacos

Empanadas

Tamales

BRAZIL

Brazilian food is a tasty blend of flavors from different cultures. The native people frequently cooked with cassava, a starchy root vegetable shaped like a carrot with a rough brown skin. Cassava can be dried and ground into tapioca flour and then used to make bread, pancakes, and porridge. In addition to cassava, native people also ate pineapples and other tropical fruit that grow well in Brazil's warm climate, as well as beans, cashews, Brazil nuts, and fish.

Portuguese conquerors arrived on Brazil's shores in 1500 and brought some of their favorite foods with them—dried and salted cod (a type of fish), cheese, olives, almonds, garlic, and onions. Later, West African people arrived in Brazil and introduced such foods as okra, black-eyed peas, and dried shrimp.

Today, Brazilian chefs combine food traditions to make tasty barbecued meats, fish stews with okra, pork and bean dishes, and sweet tapioca puddings. When you eat Brazilian food, you can taste a mix of South American, European, and African food cultures!

★ POPULAR BRAZILIAN FOODS ★

AÇAI BOWL (ah-SAH-ee): puree of açai fruit, topped with fruits, nuts, or coconut

COXINHA (coh-SHEEN-ya): shredded chicken, fried in dough

FEIJOADA (fay-JU-ada): stew of black beans, sausage, and pork

MOQUECA (moh-KAY-kah): fish stew with tomatoes and onions

PÃO DE QUEIJO (POW de KAY-joo): CHEESE ROLLS

(8 servings)

INGREDIENTS
- 3 cups tapioca flour (available at your local grocery store)
- 1-1/2 cups shredded Parmesan cheese
- 1/2 teaspoon baking powder
- 1 teaspoon salt
- 2 eggs (room temperature)
- 2/3 cup olive oil
- 1-1/4 cups milk

INSTRUCTIONS
- Preheat oven to 400 degrees F.
- Mix all ingredients in a blender until smooth.
- Pour into the eight cups of a standard nonstick muffin pan. Fill each cup two-thirds full.
- Bake 20 to 25 minutes, or until puffy and golden brown.

Coxinha

Moqueca

Açai Bowl

Brazil

AMAZON Rainforest

AMAZON River

ATLANTIC Ocean

BRASILIA ★

IGUAZU FALLS

RIO de JANEIRO

CHRIST the REDEEMER

COPACABANA Beach

CASSAVA

BRAZIL NUTS

CASHEWS

AÇAI

CATTLE

SOY BEANS

SPAIN

Spanish cuisine is tied to Spain's history of invasions. When the Romans invaded Spain thousands of years ago, they planted groves of olive trees, and now olives and olive oil show up in many Spanish recipes. Hundreds of years after the Roman invasion, people from North Africa invaded and introduced almonds, oranges, lemons, and sugarcane, all of which are still important in Spanish cooking today. These conquerors from North Africa also grew rice. Paella, Spain's well-known rice dish, is cooked with saffron, a spice that was also brought into Spain from North Africa.

The Spanish diet would expand once again after Christopher Columbus sailed to the Americas and claimed land for Spain. This time, the Spanish were the conquerors. Columbus and other Spanish conquistadors (conquerors) returned to Spain with potatoes, tomatoes, peppers, and cocoa beans on their ships. Many signature Spanish dishes today include these foods.

POPULAR SPANISH FOODS

GAZPACHO (gaz-PA-choh): cold, puréed tomato-based soup

PAELLA (pie-YAY-ah): rice stew

PISTO (PEE-stoh): stewed tomatoes, eggplant, zucchini, and peppers

TORTILLA DE PATATES (tor-TEE-yah day pah-TAH-tays): potato omelet

HAM AND CHEESE TAPAS (TAH-pas): APPETIZER
(6 servings)

INGREDIENTS
- 6 slices of Serrano ham (or other thinly-sliced variety)
- 6 thin slices of Manchego cheese
- 6 Spanish olives, pitted

INSTRUCTIONS
- Place a slice of cheese on a slice of ham and roll them up.
- Stick a toothpick through the ham and cheese.
- Add an olive to the toothpick.
- Serve on a small dish or cutting board.

Tortilla de Patates

Paella

Gazpacho

Spain

BAY of BISCAY

AS CATEDRAIS

PYRENEES

LAS MEDULAS

ATLANTIC
Ocean

★ MADRID

MOSQUE of CORDOBA

CANARY
Islands

MEDITERRANEAN
Sea

OLIVES

ANCHOVIES

BANANAS

TOMATOES

SARDINES

RICE

ORANGES

FRANCE

Ooh la la—we're in France! French cuisine developed over centuries into what it is today thanks to the work of some incredibly talented and creative French chefs. One chef, Marie-Antoine Carême, was born into a poor family in 1784 and started working as a kitchen boy at age ten. He became famous for creating pastry sculptures that dazzled French royalty and for inventing special sauces that transformed French cooking.

Today, French chefs incorporate cheese, truffles, and herbs into their cooking. France has over five hundred types of cheese, including Brie and Camembert, two soft cheeses that you may have tasted. Truffles, a type of mushroom that grows underground, are prized for their strong, earthy flavor and are used in many French dishes. And to add even more savory flavor, chefs use herbs in almost everything! Thyme, rosemary, sage, and oregano are added to soups, stews, and sauces, or used as a rub for grilled meat. You can probably find some of these herbs in your kitchen cabinet! Bon appétit!

POPULAR FRENCH FOODS

CASSOULET (CA-soo-lay): duck and bean stew

CRÊPES (CREPs): thin pancakes rolled with sweet or savory fillings

MOULES FRITES (MOOL freet): mussels in broth, with French fries

POT-AU-FEU (POT-oh-fuh): beef and vegetable stew

CROQUE MONSIEUR (CROK muh-see-YUH): BROILED HAM AND CHEESE SANDWICH
(1 serving)

INGREDIENTS
- 2 slices of bread, toasted
- Butter or mustard
- 1 slice of ham
- 1 slice of Gruyère cheese
- 1/4 cup of shredded cheese

INSTRUCTIONS
- Set the oven to broil.
- Place a slice of toast on a cookie sheet.
- Spread it with butter or mustard.
- Add a slice of ham to the piece of toast.
- Top the ham with a slice of cheese.
- Cover the ham and cheese with the other slice of toast.
- Butter the top piece of toast and coat it with shredded cheese.
- Broil until the cheese melts and bubbles and begins to turn light brown.

Crêpes

Pot-Au-Feu

Moules Frites

ITALY

You may have heard that the Italians are responsible for making pizza famous, but did you know that pizza started out as a flat disc of bread roasted on stone? People didn't begin adding basic toppings like olive oil, tomato, garlic, and rosemary until centuries later. Legend has it that in 1889 King Umberto and Queen Margherita of Italy visited Naples—a city now famous for pizza—and while they were there, Chef Raffael Esposito invented a new pizza with colorful toppings in green, white, and red to match the Italian flag. He named it for the queen, and only since then—or so goes the legend—have we had the pleasure of eating a cheesy, basil-topped Margherita pizza. Historians have questioned this famous tale, but true or false, it's still a great story!

In case you think Italy has only pizza to offer, let's look at its other specialties. If you've ever been to an Italian restaurant, you know that there's a whole section on the menu for pasta. Pasta is made from Durum wheat that is grown in southern Italy. In northern Italy, Arborio rice is harvested, which is what chefs use to make risotto, a creamy rice dish. Like France, Italy is also famous for its cheese. There are over four hundred kinds of cheeses in Italy. Many of those end up on top of—you guessed it—*pizza*!

POPULAR ITALIAN FOODS

CACCIUCCO (ca-CHEW-coh): seafood stew

CACIO E PEPE (CA-cho ee PEP-ay): pasta with cheese and pepper

GNOCCHI (nee-OH-kee): potato dumplings

RISOTTO (ree-ZOH-toh): Arborio rice slow-cooked with broth

PESTO:
BASIL AND CHEESE SAUCE
(4 servings)

INGREDIENTS
- 1 cup fresh basil leaves
- 1 clove garlic, crushed or minced
- 3 tablespoons pine nuts
- 1/3 cup grated Parmesan cheese
- 1/3 cup olive oil
- 1/2 teaspoon salt

INSTRUCTIONS
- Put all ingredients in a blender.
- Blend until smooth. If too thick, add more olive oil.
- Eat as a dip for raw vegetables or serve over warm pasta or rice.

WANT TO TRY THIS? Traditionally, Italians hand-blend their pesto with a mortar and pestle. Try that if you're feeling strong!

Gnocchi

Risotto

Cacciucco

GREECE

Greek cuisine dates back to ancient times. The oldest cookbook in the world is from Greece. More than two thousand years ago, the author of that cookbook, Archestratus, advised people not to cover up the natural flavor of foods with heavy seasoning. In the book, he praises foods like seafood, bread, and honey, all of which are still popular in Greece today.

Much of Greek food culture is tied to its mountainous geography where, due to the well-drained soil and sunny climate, olives, grapes, and almonds grow well. Goats and sheep graze on the hillsides, and from their milk, people make cheese and yogurt. Greece is also surrounded by the Mediterranean and Aegean Seas, which is why fish and other seafood are a big part of the cuisine. Today, Greek cooking is still known for its simple, fresh, and lightly seasoned foods.

POPULAR GREEK FOODS

DOLMADES (dol-MA-days): grape leaves rolled around herbed rice, and boiled

KALAMARI (ka-la-MAH-ree): squid pieces coated in flour and fried

MOUSSAKA (MOO-sa-ka): casserole made of eggplant and ground beef or lamb

SPANAKOPITA (span-ah-KOH-pita): spinach and Feta cheese baked in flaky pastry

TZATZIKI (tzah-DZEE-kee): CUCUMBER AND YOGURT SALAD
(2–3 servings)

INGREDIENTS
- 1 cucumber, peeled and coarsely grated
- 1-1/2 cups Greek yogurt
- 2 tablespoons extra virgin olive oil
- 1 clove garlic, minced
- 1/2 teaspoon salt
- 1 tablespoon fresh dill, chopped
- Squeeze of lemon juice

INSTRUCTIONS
- Pat the grated cucumber with paper towels to soak up moisture.
- In a bowl, stir cucumber with yogurt, oil, garlic, and salt.
- Add the dill and a squeeze of lemon juice on top.
- Serve with pita bread or grilled meats.

Moussaka

Dolmades

Kalamari

MOROCCO

Morocco is bordered by the Mediterranean Sea to the north, and the Atlantic Ocean to the west and south. This means that people in Morocco have always had easy access to fish. Berbers, the native people of Morocco, cooked with wheat, maize, and legumes, which all grow well in Morocco's fertile soil. When desert tribesmen from Arabia conquered the land and settled in Morocco, they brought with them such spices as cinnamon, ginger, saffron, and cumin. All of these spices are still used in Moroccan cooking today. The tribesmen also introduced a sweet-and-sour cooking style that you can taste in Morocco's favorite dishes, including tagine (stew), and couscous (steamed grain) topped with meat and vegetables.

Alongside their meals, Moroccan people love drinking mint tea. This tradition started in the 1800s when British merchants brought tea from China to Morocco. People loved it and began brewing it with Moroccan spearmint and other Moroccan herbs. Each cup of tea is a reminder of the blended traditions that make up Moroccan culture.

POPULAR MOROCCAN FOODS

BESSARA (bi-SAR-a): fava bean soup

COUSCOUS (COOS-coos): steamed semolina, with meat and vegetables

TAGINE (ta-JEEN): stew cooked in an earthenware pot

ZAALOUK (za-LOUK): smoked eggplant dip

SHLATA CHIZO (SHLAH-da KEE-zoo): ZESTY CARROT-ORANGE SALAD

(3–4 servings)

INGREDIENTS

- 2 carrots, finely grated
- 6 dates, chopped
- 2 oranges peeled, separated, and chopped
- Juice of one lemon
- 1 tablespoon honey
- Pinch of salt
- 1/4 teaspoon cinnamon
- 1/4 teaspoon cumin
- 1/4 cup olive oil

INSTRUCTIONS

- In a bowl, whisk together the lemon juice, honey, salt, spices, and olive oil.
- Stir in the grated carrots. Let sit for 5 minutes.
- Mix in the chopped dates and oranges.
- Serve in a bowl and sprinkle with a dash of cinnamon.

OPTIONAL: Top with parsley.

Tagine

Bessara

Zaalouk

ETHIOPIA

There are more than eighty different religious groups in Ethiopia, and the cuisine is just as diverse! Orthodox Christians in Ethiopia have about two hundred days of fasting a year. They do not eat meat or dairy products on those days. Similarly, the Muslim population—in line with religious beliefs—does not eat pork. These religious traditions have resulted in a cuisine that includes a variety of meatless recipes.

Chickpeas, lentils, and split peas are used in many Ethiopian dishes. These foods are spiced with berbere, a blend of chili pepper, garlic, ginger, cumin, and coriander powders. Most Ethiopian meals start with injera, a spongy pancake made from teff, which is a tiny seed from an ancient grass that is ground into flour. People pile vegetable or meat wot (stew) on top of injera and eat the whole thing with their fingers. You can taste Ethiopia's diverse traditions in every spicy bite!

★POPULAR ETHIOPIAN FOODS★

DORO WOT (DO-ro wot): spicy chicken stew

HARIRA (HAH-rear-ah): spicy bean soup

MISIR ALICHA WOT (mis-SEER a-LEE-cha wot): green lentil stew

SHIRO WOT (shee-RO wot): ground lentil and chickpea stew

INJERA (in-JAIR-ah): SPONGY FLATBREAD (EASY STYLE*)
(4 servings)

INGREDIENTS
- 1 cup teff flour (gluten free; available at your local health food store)
- 1/2 teaspoon salt
- 1 teaspoon baking powder
- 1-1/2 cups club soda

INSTRUCTIONS
- Combine teff flour, salt, and baking soda in a bowl.
- Stir in club soda to make a thin batter.
- Heat a nonstick frying pan.
- Ladle the batter into the pan to make one large, thin pancake.
- Cover the pan to keep moisture in.
- Cook 2 to 3 minutes. The batter will bubble up, pop, and dry. (Do not flip the pancake.)
- Slide the injera onto a plate and serve with stewed meat and vegetables.
- Eat with your fingers, scooping up meat and vegetables with the injera.

FERMENT YOUR INJERA? The traditional recipe uses water, not club soda, and allows the batter to ferment and bubble up for a few days before it is cooked.

Doro Wot

Harira

Shiro Wot

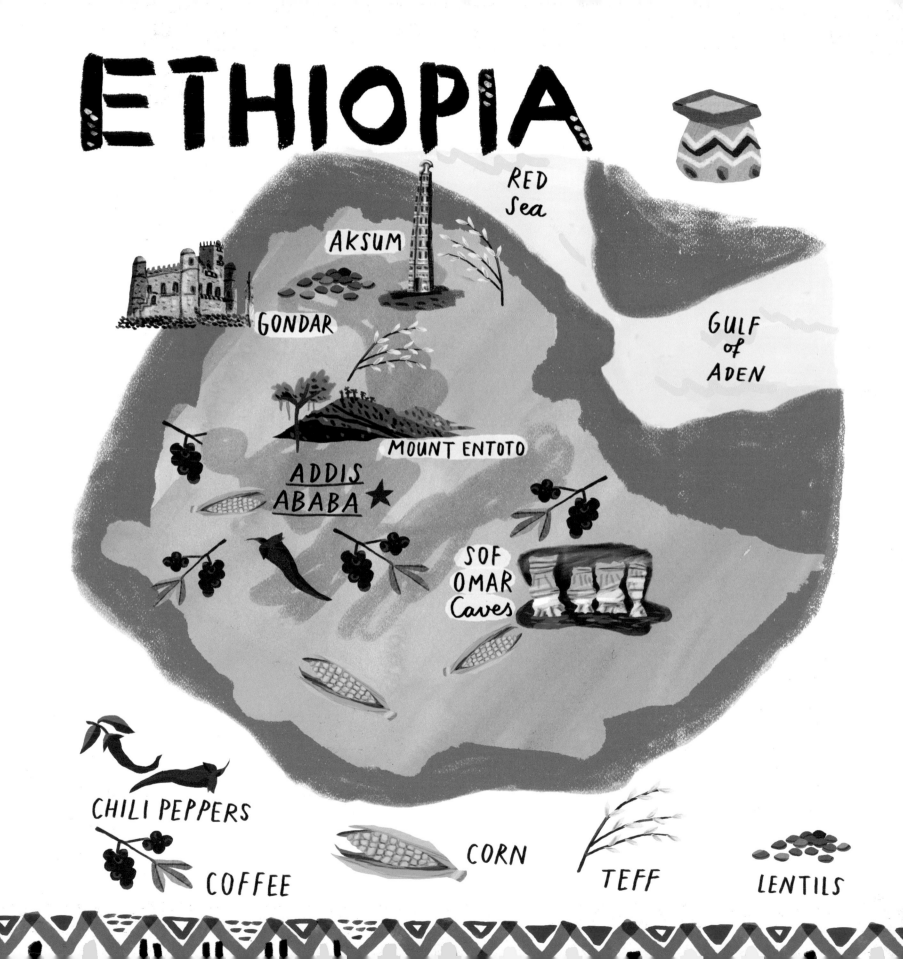

ISRAEL

Israel's cuisine is a blend of old traditions from the Middle East, North Africa, and Europe. For over a thousand years, people in the region have eaten traditional Middle Eastern foods such as wheat, legumes, olives, grapes, figs, lamb, and dairy products. Hummus (pureed chickpeas) and falafel (deep-fried chickpea balls) are dishes that date back to ancient times, as does shawarma (slow-grilled meat). If you've ever been to a Middle Eastern restaurant, you've probably seen these foods on the menu.

When Europeans migrated to Israel, they brought with them such foods as veal schnitzel (meat from a young cow, breaded and pan-fried), goulash (spiced stew), and latkes (potato fritters or pancakes), to name just a few. People from North Africa also migrated to Israel and brought dishes that are now popular. Couscous and shakshuka (eggs poached in spicy tomato sauce) are two examples. When you sit down for a meal of Israeli food, you can explore culinary traditions from three different continents!

POPULAR ISRAELI FOODS

BABA GANOUSH (baba ga-NOOSH): cooked eggplant spread

FALAFEL (fa-LA-fell): deep-fried chickpea balls

LABNEH (LAB-nuh): soft, creamy cheese made from yogurt

TABOULEH (ta-BOO-lay): parsley and bulgur wheat salad

HUMMUS (HUM-us): PUREED CHICKPEA DISH
(3–4 servings)

INGREDIENTS
• 1 can of cooked chickpeas
• 2 teaspoons lemon juice
• 8 tablespoons olive oil
• 3 tablespoons tahini
• 1 clove of garlic, minced
• 1 teaspoon salt

INSTRUCTIONS
• Mix all ingredients in a blender until very smooth.
• If the hummus is too thick, add more olive oil.
• Scoop your hummus into a serving bowl.
• Drizzle with olive oil and serve with pita bread and raw vegetables.

Baba Ganoush

Falafel

Tabouleh

INDIA

India's diverse cuisine is influenced by many religious customs. The Hindu and Jain people in India, for example, believe in *ahimsa,* or nonviolence, even to animals. Because of this belief, many people do not eat meat. Their meals are instead typically made up of rice with vegetables and legumes that are often spiced with black pepper, chili pepper, ginger, cumin, coriander, and cardamom. One popular vegetable dish is aloo gobi, a savory potato and cauliflower mix. Muslim people in India also follow certain rules when it comes to food. Their religion allows them to eat a variety of meats but not pork. They often prepare beef or chicken tandoori style, which means cooked in a clay oven. Chicken tikka masala is a popular meat dish, made up of bite-size chicken pieces stewed in a creamy, tomato-based curry sauce that is then served over rice.

People in India may practice many different religions, but when it comes to eating, most people use their right hand. When you make Indian food at home, try eating it with your fingers to get the full cultural experience!

★POPULAR INDIAN FOODS★

BIRIYANI (BEER-ee-an-ee): fried rice

DAL (dahl): spiced lentils

MATTAR PANEER (MA-tar pa-NEER): peas and Indian cheese in a sauce

SAMOSA (sa-MO-sa): pastry filled with vegetables or meat and then fried

---

BANANA LASSI (LAH-see): INDIAN YOGURT DRINK
(2 servings)

INGREDIENTS:
- 2 ripe bananas, peeled
- 1 cup plain yogurt
- 1/2 cup milk
- 1 tablespoon honey
- Pinch of cinnamon and cardamom

INSTRUCTIONS
- Combine ingredients in a blender until smooth.
- Serve at room temperature or over ice in your favorite glass, and sip through a straw if you'd like.

Samosa

Biriyani

Mattar Paneer

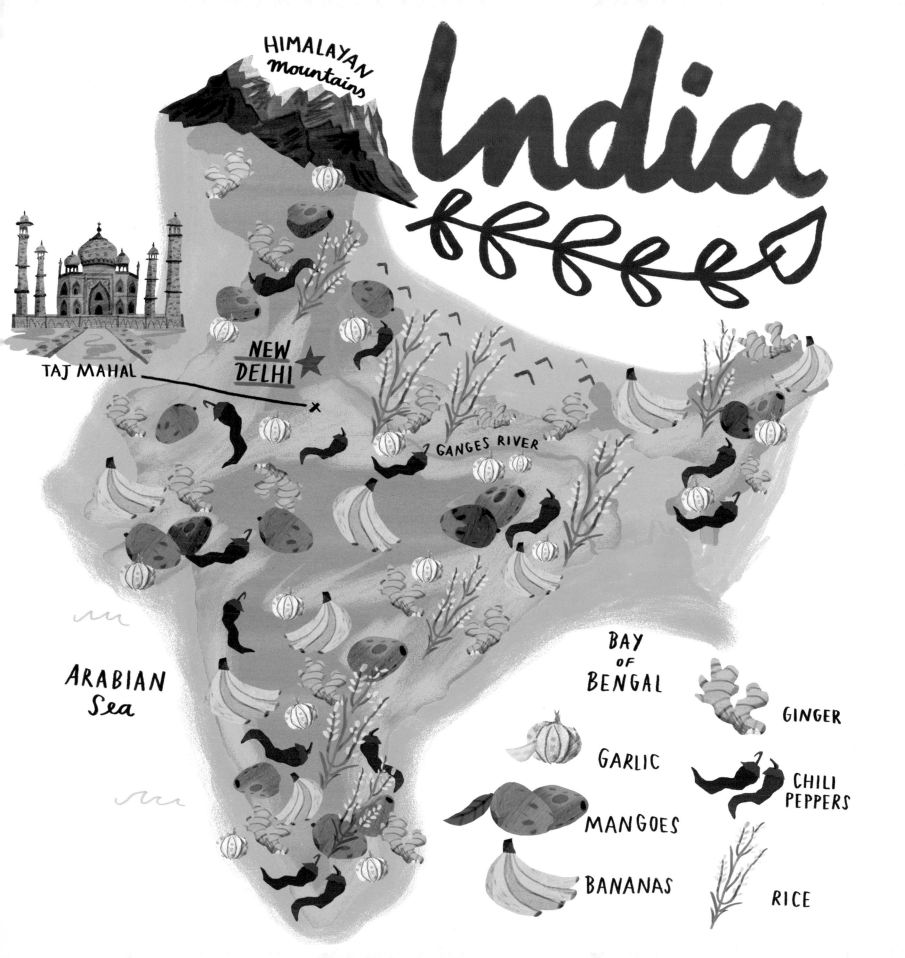

THAILAND

Thailand's cuisine begins with rice and spice. More than a thousand years ago, the T'ai people migrated from southern China to what is now Thailand, and they planted rice paddies throughout the valleys. Today people in Thailand eat rice at almost every meal. Traders from India brought cinnamon, clove, cumin, and cardamom into Thailand, and chefs use these spices for curried meat, fish, and vegetable dishes. Portuguese and Spanish traders later introduced chili peppers from the Americas, thus giving Thai food its signature heat. In the 1700s, Chinese immigrants added noodles, soy sauce, and tofu to Thai cuisine and introduced a stir-fry cooking style. Today Thailand's chefs carefully choose spices and local products to balance five essential flavors in their cooking: salty, sweet, sour, bitter, and spicy. They add fish sauce or shrimp paste to create a salty flavor and then they balance it with palm sugar. They use vinegar, lime, or tamarind (a fruit) for a sour flavor, and bitter melon or greens for a more bitter taste. Finally, chefs toss chili peppers, peppercorns, and ginger into their recipes to make the food spicy. In sauces, that heat is balanced with creamy coconut milk. Put all these flavors together and you get food that is both bold and rich!

POPULAR THAI FOODS

JOK (JOKE): savory rice porridge

KAENG KHIAO WAN KAI (gang KYAH wan kai): sweet green curry chicken

TOM YUM GOONG (tom yum GOONG): shrimp and vegetable soup

YUM WOON SEN (yum woon SEN): glass noodle salad

VEGETABLE PAD THAI (pad TIE): PAN-FRIED RICE NOODLES WITH VEGETABLES

(4 servings)

INGREDIENTS
- 8 oz. dry rice noodles
- 1 tablespoon soy sauce
- 2 tablespoons sesame oil
- 1 tablespoon rice vinegar
- 1 teaspoon honey
- 1 clove of garlic, minced
- Oil, for frying
- 1 egg
- 3/4 cup bean sprouts
- 1 scallion, chopped
- 2 tablespoons chopped peanuts (optional)

INSTRUCTIONS
- Soak rice noodles in warm water until slightly soft. Drain well.
- Stir together soy sauce, sesame oil, rice vinegar, and honey, and set sauce aside.
- Sauté garlic in a pan with a little vegetable oil. Crack egg into the pan, and stir gently.
- Add bean sprouts and scallions and stir.
- Add noodles and sauce and stir everything together.
- Sprinkle with chopped peanuts (optional). Serve and enjoy!

OPTIONAL: Authentic Pad Thai includes chili peppers for spice.

Kaeng Khiao Wan Kai

Tom Yum Goong

Yum Woon Sen

Thailand

CASHEWS

CHILI PEPPERS

COCONUTS

SQUID

CRABS

LIMES

RICE

CATFISH

MEKONG River

AYUTTHAYA

BANGKOK

ANDAMAN Sea

FLOATING MARKET

GULF of THAILAND

CHINA

Chinese cuisine has been around for thousands of years and is tied to the importance of family in Chinese culture. Ancient recipes have been passed down from generation to generation, and almost all Chinese food can be traced back to one of China's eight great cooking traditions. These traditions share basic ingredients like garlic, ginger, scallions, and sesame oil, but they also have unique qualities. The Sichuan style is famous for its spice, which comes from chili peppers and Sichuan peppercorns. The Quangdong style is known for dim sum, a brunch meal made up of small platters of food, usually either steamed or fried. The Jiangsu cooking style incorporates seafood in soups and stews, whereas Anhui cooking tends to call for forest herbs and bamboo shoots. Stir-fried dishes in Hunan are known for being spicy and sour, whereas Fujian cooking is famous for seasoning food with fermented fish sauce and shrimp paste. Shandong chefs often serve wheat noodles and meat-filled buns, and finally, Zhejiang cooking is famous for its sweet desserts made from sticky rice. Today Chinese families continue to cook and eat together, and by doing so, keep their ancient food traditions alive.

POPULAR CHINESE FOODS

CHAR SIU BAO (CHAR show bow): steamed pork-filled buns

CONGEE (CON-gee): soupy rice breakfast dish

MAPO DOFU (MA-po DO-fu): spicy beef and tofu dish

PEKING DUCK (PAY-king duck): roasted duck specialty

SESAME NOODLES: WHEAT NOODLES WITH A SALTY SESAME SAUCE
(4 servings)

INGREDIENTS
- 12 oz. Chinese noodles (available in the Asian food section of your local grocery store)
- 1/4 cup soy sauce
- 1 teaspoon garlic, minced
- 1 tablespoon honey
- 3 tablespoons sesame oil
- 2 tablespoons rice vinegar
- 1 tablespoon smooth peanut butter
- 1 tablespoon sesame paste or tahini

INSTRUCTIONS
- Cook noodles according to the package instructions.
- Drain in a colander and rinse in cold water so the noodles don't stick.
- In a bowl, whisk all other ingredients until smooth.
- Pour the sauce over noodles and stir. Serve cold or at room temperature.

OPTIONAL: Add chopped peanuts, shredded carrots, or chopped scallions.

Char Siu Bao

Mapo Dofu

Peking Duck

CHINA

FORBIDDEN CITY

GREAT WALL

BEIJING

Shandong

Jiangsu

Zhejiang

TERRACOTTA WARRIORS

Sichuan

Anhui

EAST CHINA Sea

MOUNT EVEREST

Hunan

Fujian

Guangdong

SOUTH CHINA Sea

PEACHES

SUNFLOWER SEEDS

TEA

RICE

DATES

JAPAN

One of the most important aspects of Japanese cooking is presentation. In a bowl of rice, noodles, or broth, Japanese chefs carefully arrange small, colorful portions of fish, meat, and vegetables. Because Japan is an island nation, chefs often cook with fish or other seafood. They grill fish, batter-fry it, or use it raw in sushi. Chefs balance flavors with such seasonings as grated ginger, soy sauce, horseradish, and vinegar. Once plated, the finished dishes often look like works of art.

Japanese people might not all be culinary artists at home, but they still appreciate the same delicate flavors that chefs enjoy. They often eat a bowl of white rice with miso (soybean paste) soup and add some tsukemono (pickled vegetables) and ginger. In winter, people put their own personal touches on oden, a traditional hearty stew, by adding to it such ingredients as fish cakes, tofu, radish slivers, noodles, and hard-boiled eggs. Japanese cooking is artful and uniquely satisfying!

POPULAR JAPANESE FOODS

COLD SOBA (SOH-ba): buckwheat noodles with soy sauce dip

SUSHI (SOO-shee): vinegar-flavored sticky rice topped with fish or vegetables or rolled in seaweed

TEMPURA (tem-POOR-ah): battered and fried fish, meat, or vegetables

YAKITORI CHICKEN (YA-kee-tor-ee): grilled chicken on a skewer

MISO (MEE-soh) SOUP: SOUP MADE OF SOYBEAN PASTE AND SEAWEED BROTH
(6 servings)

INGREDIENTS
- 4 cups boiling water, divided
- 1 teaspoons instant dashi powder (available in the Asian food section of your local grocery store; if unavailable, replace water with seafood or chicken broth.)
- 1/4 cup cubed tofu
- 1/4 cup miso paste (available in the Asian food section of your local grocery store or refrigerated in health-food stores)

INSTRUCTIONS
- In a pot, dissolve dashi powder in 3 cups boiling water.
- Add cubed tofu and stir.
- Let simmer on low heat for 2 minutes. Turn off heat. Let the water cool a bit.
- In a bowl, dissolve miso paste in one cup of hot water.
- Add the miso liquid to the rest of the broth in the pot and stir well.
- Serve in small bowls.

OPTIONAL: Top with chopped scallions or grated carrots.

Sushi

Yakitori Chicken

Tempura

Japan

TUNA

SEA URCHIN

TEA

APPLES

DAIKON

RICE

CITRUS

BLOWFISH

Sea of
JAPAN

KYOTO

PACIFIC
Ocean

TOKYO

MOUNT FUJI

KUMAMOTO
Castle

AROUND THE WORLD AND HOME AGAIN

Now that you've made your way around the world, it's time to start cooking at home. There's nothing better than experimenting with flavors and adding your own touch to age-old recipes. Once you've perfected a dish so it tastes just the way you like it, invite some friends over and share! Throw a potluck party and ask each guest to bring a favorite dish. On a map, mark the country where each dish originated. This way, you'll continue to explore the world and its many flavors.

Bon appétit!

Chī hǎo hē hǎo!
吃好喝好!

Happy eating!

Mälkam məgəb!
መልካም ምግብ!

Buon appetito!

ITADAKIMASU!
いただきます!

¡Buen provecho!

31

GLOSSARY

Artful: showing art or skill

Broil: to cook directly under heat

Colonist: a person who colonizes or settles in a new country

Climate: general weather conditions

Continent: one of the seven great divisions of land

Cuisine: style of cooking

Culinary: related to cooking

Culture: knowledge and values shared by a society

Curry: a blend of ground spices or a dish seasoned with a blend of ground spices

Custom: the usual way of doing something

Dairy: related to milk, butter, and cheese

Diverse: different from one another

Herb: a plant used for seasoning food

Immigrant: a person who moves to a new country to live in

Flavor: the way food tastes in your mouth

Geography: the physical features of a place

Generation: the period of time between the birth of parents and birth of their children

Heritage: traditions and beliefs coming from the past

Legumes: group of foods that includes peas, beans, and peanuts

Mortar and pestle: a heavy bowl and a blunt club used for crushing or grinding food

Migrate: to move from one country or place to another

Native: born in a particular place or country

Savory: having a spicy or salty taste

Seasoning: herbs or spices added to flavor food

Spice: a plant product with a strong taste (like pepper or nutmeg) used to flavor food

Tradition: thoughts, actions, and behaviors that are repeated over time

Traditional: having to do with the way things have been done over a long period of time

Variety: a number or collection of different things